We Love a Ukulele

Tall Tales from Care Homes

with love

Ellen

ISBN: 978-1-913218-64-5

With heartfelt thanks to Minnie Sandbach
for her beautiful illustrations

For every care worker who selflessly gives
their expertise and love to the elderly
through caring every day

We Love a Ukulele

Tall Tales from Care Homes

Songs are etched into the minds of a generation and no matter how far away these old lives have disappeared to, or what reality exists for them now, a piece of life, of love, a time and memory is shared within a song.

I sing no war songs.

"Is that all there is?
If that's all there is my friend
Then let's keep dancing..."

A wobbly jelly bum is the first thing I see. Striped pyjamas hang around his skinny ankles and strings of colourless, unwashed hair lay limp on his shoulders. His eyes are fixed on the jug of orange juice he's sloshing onto the carpet. As he stretches out to put the empty jug back on the nightstand the tangle of sheets strewn about the floor trips him up and he falls face down, wibbly wobbly jelly out of control.

"I'll be back in two seconds, Mr Hosking. Don't move!" Not much danger of that, I think.

Nurse Hamm hurries me further down the hallway to the lounge. A tiny bird-woman is talking to an over-stuffed furry Jack Russell named Perkins whose feet have been wedged under the glass door on the inside, and no amount of pushing from our side will budge it. Nurse Hamm's chest glistens with sweat, her sumo wrestling arms a force to be reckoned with, but even she has to admit defeat. I wonder how Mr Hosking is faring in his sheets, the promised "I'll be back!" well past. About to give the bird-woman a safety-briefing earful, Nurse Hamm is interrupted by screams echoing from a room further away.

"I'll be back in two seconds, Evelyn, and I want you and Perkins back in your chair pronto!"

The glance of desperation she throws at me smacks of the addict who has just realised the Valium is still sitting by the teapot on the kitchen bench. She takes off towards the scream, no doubt hoping she'll bump into a drug dealer skulking in the hallway en route. I smile through the glass at Evelyn and she points to Perkins.

"Perkins is starving! He was trying to eat his own foot."

A wizened man creeps up behind Evelyn and seems to sniff her ear. She swats him absent-mindedly and like a moth not long for this world he flutters away. Nurse Hamm reappears and quips,

"We do our best. I love my job but sometimes I could throttle them, honestly."

A stern looking older nurse appears out of nowhere on the other side of the door and heaves Evelyn aside like a sack of sand, at the same time releasing Perkins from his trauma.

I'm in another era now. Wedged between the television and a dead plant I'll spend the next hour entertaining the residents who have been wheeled in and locked in place for the day. A dozen or so sleepy bodies line the room, heads slumped at all angles on chests wet with dribble or dangling like dead weights upside down over the backs of wheelchairs. Their shrunken dry mouths are wide open like chicks waiting to be fed. A few stare blankly at something only they can see. Limbless dolls and ragged bears lay forgotten beneath a sea of Zimmer frames, wilting plants struggle to survive in stifling heat, and thermal-vested residents shiver in a constant winter. One snoring fellow's teeth have half fallen out and he's making a great effort to get them back by trying to eat his own chin. Some of the women – they're mostly women in these places - chat to the carpet and the men look as though they'd rather be in a prisoner of war camp than be captive here. This is my audience: eyes stare past me into distant forevers; frail bodies seem to walk right through me, patience long gone with memory. There isn't a lot of interaction with those who have dementia but bless their souls, there's recognition in the music and that, I tell you, fills my heart.

Deborah, Ivy's daughter

"We were lucky to find this place for Mum. It's terribly expensive but worth it not to have the worry. Of her falling or hurting herself I mean. It's a charming place - one of the best homes around, I believe. But hideously expensive! There are lots of personal touches that show the thought that's gone into making the residents feel at home. Like the photographs on each door. I gave them a photo of Mum from the Blue Danube cruise she took in 1980. That was one of her happiest holidays, but before she got her new teeth so her mouth looks like an angry prune unfortunately. There's a label stuck on it that says "Ivy Booth at Sea!" and a few bullet points listing her likes and dislikes, hobbies and things. Actually, there are only dislikes because she couldn't think of one thing she liked. She hates the intrusion. "It's like the loopy wing of a home for nosy parkers!" She's got care 24/7 and a swivel stool in her bath. And the food looks easy to chew, which is important isn't it? Mind you, she's lost her appetite, the nurses say. She stays in her room mostly but then she's never been very social, which is a shame because there are so many interesting old folk here whom I'm sure she'd get on with if only she'd make the effort. One of us visits at least once a week, although my two brothers are a bit hit and miss. I come every week of course. She keeps asking when she's going home. I think it's the start of Alzheimer's. But they're equipped for that here as well. Dementia, I mean. So, we're – she's very lucky.   Her house sold in a fortnight but we haven't mentioned it.   We don't want her to think she's got no home to go to. No, all in all it's been the right decision. For her, I mean."

Ivy

"It's a gloomy Tuesday and she's sat there on the other side of my living room. My daughter, Deborah. We normally share the sofa. She's fiddling with her phone and tugging at her hair like she's always done when she's anxious. "Are you alright, love?" I say. "Yes!" she shouts at me. "Well no, no I'm not, Mum! This is very hard for me so I'm just going to have to come out and say it. Alright? The thing is, you see, the thing is I haven't got the time to keep looking in on you like this every day, Mum, and you need someone to check on you constantly and it's not fair on me really, is it? With everything else that's going on in my life, is it? Rupert's lost his job and the boys are no help, are they? I mean, they don't lift a finger to help, do they? So, the thing is - well you see, I've been making enquiries about a lovely rest home for you. Somewhere you'll make friends and be looked after... where you won't have to worry." "But I don't worry! I'm perfectly fine, love," I try to reassure her and stop her pulling all her hair out. "No, no, no you're not, Mum! You're fine as long as I can keep driving the ten-mile round trip every day to check on you but I'm worn out! You're – it's a huge worry for me and it's not really fair, is it? I think you should give it some thought, don't you? The boys agree. Try not to be selfish, Mum. I've got some lovely brochures here I want you to look at. Lovely, lovely, pretty rest homes with pretty gardens and your own pretty bathroom with a swivel bath seat and shiny silver safety poles." She pokes about in her bag and produces a pile of glossy brochures like they're the winning tickets in the lottery. "Anyway, I have to pick up the twins but have a flick through these and see if there's anything you fancy and we can talk about it next time, ok?" And she's out the door before the brochures have hit the table.

Something I fancy? Like choosing a hat. Anyway, I'm still trying to imagine the silver safety poles when one of these homes calls to ask what day I'd like to view the room that's become available. The woman on the phone, chirpy as a robin, says this as though the former occupant has just popped off to a tango convention in Barcelona. I tell her I shan't be needing the room thank you very much and I suggest she lets the former occupant's body get cold before tossing another poor soul on the conveyor belt! Unfortunately, they check with my daughter just to make sure I'm "fit" enough to make that kind of decision. Obviously I'm not. Because here I am."

"Gonna take a sentimental journey
to renew old memories…"

Never ask if there's a special request. There's always one whose musical taste time warped around 1914 and wants to hear 'My Sweetheart Went Down with the Ship', or 'Joan of Arc They Are Calling You'. And if I don't know one of these songs from that era, of which there are over two hundred on Wikipedia alone, a lot of sulking goes on. "We like a song that rhymes!" I love singing all the old standards and am always delighted how many words the residents - and surprisingly those with dementia too - remember. Fred Astaire and Ginger Rogers, Frank Sinatra and Judy Garland are sure winners. Sometimes I'm dumbfounded by a Merle Haggard fan whose mother used to hum 'Misery and Gin' to the kids while she was hanging out the washing. All of these requests come with a history that has often been told many (truly many!) times before. The mention of Doris Day brings a spark to their eyes and on hearing the first few notes of 'Que Sera Sera' they're off! I can count on a whole choir. Many of these music lovers have developed the art of mouthing the lyrics to a song they've never heard. Always a syllable behind, they stare at my lips and imitate me without a sound, heads nodding and slippers tapping out of time with the beat. There's a huge sense of satisfaction when they get to the end. "Oh, that was nice," they'll say. "Imagine me remembering all those words!"

Alice hobbles over on her walking frame and stares at me for a minute, confused, trying to remember why she crossed the room. One of the young carers has been practicing her make-up skills on Alice but it's disintegrated into ugly streaks of turquoise stretching from her eyes to her ears, and smudged vibrant red lipstick that creeps up

14

the crevices to her nose and slides down to catch in the fine hairs on her chin. It's hard not to stare back in equal confusion. She suddenly comes back to the moment and we try to solve her dilemma. It goes like this:

"Here, can we sing that one, you remember, the one oh you know, the one whatsername sings? About seven trains. Likes dogs."

"Doris Day?"

"Yes. No." She hitches her skirt up above her swollen knees which look like sausages about to burst their skin. The flesh coloured nylon pop socks are too tight and I wonder how she's allowed to wear them as they must be cutting off an important blood supply.

"A female singer?" I check.

"Yes! I think."

"Is she alive?"

"Oh yes. No. I don't know."

"OK."

"Probably dead." She bobs up and down excitedly, her little purple sausage knees quivering.

"American?"

"Danced with Bob."

"She danced?"

"Yes, with Bob." She lifts her skirt higher.

"Bob?"

"Bob? Bob?"

"Judy Garland?"

"White hair."

She swishes her skirt from side to side and I'm starting to fear there's an uncanny likeness to Bette Davis in 'Whatever Happened to Baby Jane'. If she starts singing

'I've Written a Letter to Daddy' I'll call the nurse.

"Doris Day?"

"Yes! That's her!"

"...counting every mile of railroad track that takes me back..."

"Yes! That's the one!"

"The memory of all that,
No, they can't take that away from me…"

The staff calls them The Mafia. Fi and Maggie sit close together and as far away from the other residents as possible. They've come to resemble each other over the years with home-knitted cardigans buttoned rigid, large safety pins holding identical zip-up slippers snug. They have their hair "done" on the same day, set with a little Elnet to give it that salon look. Fi and Maggie deeply resent sharing the lounge with anyone else, especially dear Betty whose memory is fading in big chunks. Fi's index finger is a permanently poised pistol champing at the bit to shoot Betty down as soon as she starts to sing. Betty used to sing at the Workingmen's Club her father managed in the North of England in the 1940s and now, to Fi and Maggie's great irritation, she clearly remembers this favourite:

"I'll be loving you, always..."

Fi's finger fires through the air. "No! Betty! Betty! Do NOT sing!"

But Betty is safely caught in 1940. "With a love that's true, Always..."

George has spotted me with my microphone. "Are you here to shave me?"

Fi thwhacks the air between them with her magazine and shouts, "Shut up, George!"

"I haven't had a shave!"

Fi's voice rises to a shrill. "The lady came this morning you stupid man! Now shut up!"

Maggie has drifted into another realm entirely and puts down her crossword puzzle. She says to me, "Remember little Mary, dear? No hair? She died. Two, no – yesterday was it - or three days ago I forget. Cancer."

Fi can keep three conversations going simultaneously. "That was Monday! Sit down you awful man! Betty!"

Maggie hesitates. "No... Tuesday I think it was."

Fi stabs her pencil clean through a Sudoku square. "No, it wasn't!"

Maggie closes her eyes trying to picture the drama. "I was going upstairs and they were carrying her up... up... no, no I was going UP the stairs to fetch – something I can't remember - so she must have been coming down the stairs. My cardigan. Right past me. That's not right, is it? Dead. Right past me on the stairs."

Fi throws the Sudoku magazine on the floor in exasperation. "Well, that's life isn't it!"

Maggie sighs. "Yes, it is. All dead. And I'm eighty-seven. Brenda Sanje, in the same block as me, died of breast cancer last Friday. In her eighties she was. I saw her two weeks ago buying some crisps. She looked alright. Didn't say much, just the usual "Nice day isn't it?" A few "nice" days later she's dead. Makes you think."

I pick up Fi's magazine but as I go to put it on the side table she snatches it off me and waves it at George. "One more peep out of you and I'll thrash you with this, you silly, silly, awful man!"

Betty has drifted off to sleep and Maggie whispers, "I need a wee".

Carlo, a nurse

"My father ended up in a home like this. I used to dread visiting because I couldn't stand walking into the silence. Everyone seated around the edge of a large dreary room, facing one another. And yet no one spoke. A bit more of me broke every time I visited. My mother and I came three times a week for six months and sat mostly in silence for a couple of hours. We liked it when there was some entertainment because it relieved the pressure of having to find something to say. I like to believe my father didn't suffer. But then, how do I know? One day I helped a carer hand out the tea to distract me from Dad's awful silence. I could see how overworked everyone was too. The carer was from The Philippines and I had often admired how he did everything with such grace. He could lighten the mood in the room by suddenly sweeping a nurse off her feet and dancing in crazy ways, making the residents laugh. It was like shining a light on something they'd tucked away and forgotten years and years ago. You could almost reach out and touch their memories. I said to him, "I don't know how you do this every day. Doesn't it ever get you down, seeing this? Seeing people getting worse? No one gets better. It's tragic." "That's because you're only an observer," he said. "When you become part of their lives it's a privilege to do this. Caring for someone while they reach the end of their life is a privilege. I hate the mess. But I love everything else about being here."

Not so long after that I trained as a carer and then as a nurse. There was never any doubt in my mind after my father died that this was what I would do. I watched in awe at the way those incredible people cared for him.

They loved him, simple as that."

25

"Before the parade passes by
I'd like to put some life back into my life"

I notice the promises on the signs in front of
these care homes, usually located in a garden
at the expensive residences and concreted in
next to the wheelie bins at the more basic. The
prettiest fonts are as carefully selected as the
words: 'Stimulation Around the Clock', 'Fun
and End of Life Care', etc. Sometimes the waft
of disinfectant is so overwhelming I wonder
whose 'home-away-from-home' this mirrors?
I feel for those who are herded into lines to
face the world of daytime television that
screams at them on a mind-numbing
continuous loop. This is where I find Ruby the
next day, yelling at Judge Rinder on ITV that
he's an idiot.

"I'd like to stick my digestive up your
bum!"

Her tirade is interrupted when little Ronnie B is caught feeding his digestive to the rubber plant.

"He's put his biscuit in the plant!" cackles Molly.

"No I didn't!" says Ronnie B, wishing he knew where he could bury his soil covered hands.

Ninety-year-old Phyllis who, by her own account is a descendant of royalty, has appointed herself proxy queen of this establishment and pronounces her opinion on Ronnie B's criminal behaviour. "I think if you're capable of cruelty to plants or animals you should be put down!" she says, sounding distinctly like Edith Evans.

"I never put it in the plant!" Ronnie B is close to tears.

"My Bosey was eighteen when we made the terrible decision to put him to sleep," Phyllis continues. "My precious Bosey never wee'd on a plant. Only weeds. Very intelligent, dear Bosey. Dogs are though, aren't they? And much nicer than humans."

"My father has canaries at home," Molly chips in. "I can't remember their names only Custard."

"Beautiful Bosey was a pure-breed, which is why he was so intelligent. Mongrels should be drowned at birth," says Phyllis.

"They peck and poo on your shoulder!" Molly laughs until her eyes water and she shifts uncomfortably in her chair.

"What breed was he?" enquires a nervous Ronnie B, glad to be let off the hook over the digestive.

"Pug."

"Ugly little buggers, pugs. They can't breathe," mutters Mrs Henley from behind the rubber plant.

"Of course they breathe!" scowls Phyllis.

"No, I mean, like normal breathing. They snort!" dares Mrs Henley.

With that Phyllis snaps the vertical blind shut much the same as chopping Mrs Henley's head off and the conversation is closed. No one utters another word. Phyllis commands the velvet brocade armchair with the best view of the garden and - most importantly - has sole control of the vertical blind! Sunshine and light, by order of Phyllis.

"I need the toilet!" shouts Molly.

Judge Rinder has finished sentencing life's losers and Ruby is nodding off. I remember one of her favourite songs so I switch the TV off and start the music.

"Shut up!" hisses Mrs Henley through the rubber plant. She's in a foul mood because Phyllis had the last word on pugs. Cupping both hands over her ears she stares at me through her coke bottle lenses. "Your singing hurts my ears! Ouch! Shut up!"

Molly, who was on her way to the toilet, takes a detour on her walking frame and smashes it into the rubber plant that whips Mrs Henley in the face. "You shut up you old bitch!" screeches Molly through the leaves.

A carer hurries in and guides Molly off to the toilet whilst Mrs Henley manages to squeeze a tear that sadly doesn't escape down her cheek in time, so I'm the only one who sees it.

Katya, A Carer

"It is taking me a long time for getting used to work here. This is second home I am working in for a long time and is very nice, very clean. You cannot smell something, can you? Only the smell is lavender air fresh. I am liking the old people and some of them are very happy. The ones have no visitors that is very sad. How is possible a person have no one? You have no one is the worst thing. But we are all of us here talking to them a lot because talking to them is the best thing. Many of people stop talking to the old people because they think the old people do not understand. Old people is the same as us but also have much pain we do not see. It is so shameful for them being a baby again. Eat with a spoon or drink from a baby cup and wearing the nappies and your pants are falling down because there is nothing to holding them up. I try for make them smiling and bring a flower or one of my kids make a picture, something like that. Such a little thing make them so happy."

"Make my bed, light the light
I'll be home late tonight
Blackbird bye bye..."

When the door opens Brenda is standing right behind the smiling carer. Brenda is in her usual coat and hat, and holding her arm is Doctor Margaret in white dressing gown, stethoscope and sombrero. Doctor Margaret takes my arm too and leads us to the lounge, whispering that we're very lucky because she's giving free consultations for everyone today. As I set up, Mrs Chen approaches Doctor Margaret and punches her. Mrs Chen is taken away and everyone is given an ice-cream.

The clang clang of the tea trolley brings instant activity. Those deep in sleep open one eye – they'll wait for the tea to be poured before opening the other. Anyone mid-way to the toilet turns around (what's another 'little accident'?) in case they miss out on cake.

Cake passes the time. It is a toy boat in saucers full of slopped tea; it is disassembled crumb by dry crumb and trodden into the floral carpet or fed to dolls with painted-on mouths. Cups tremble in feeble hands though some can't manage and sip through a straw or from a baby's training cup. Sylvia downs her tea in a few gulps and until lunchtime she cradles and rocks the empty cup, humming, mesmerized:

"There, there", she says. "There, there".

Ivor arrives hot on the heels of the trolley but feigns great surprise when he's offered tea and cake. Ivor was an Ac-tor. He is tall, slim and has a shock of suspiciously blonde hair. His teeth sport chunky gold fillings, and his hands weave the air to accentuate every syllable of his soliloquy.

"Tea! And cake! Oh, how kind! Thank you, dear, sweet nurse!" he sings.

The carer, Gloria, is happy to see him. "Are you going to sing then, Ivor?" She whispers to me, "He was a famous actor!"

"No, no, no. I have far too much to do this morning. My son is coming to take me back home today!"

"He was really famous!" Gloria beams. "He was in Television. 'Z Cars' wasn't it, Ivor?"

"Now, now nurse! You will have me blushing!"

Gloria revels in Ivor's fame. She says to me, "You know that actress who was on the tele in 'Emmerdale Farm'? Years she was in it! Well, she was a burglar in this episode and Ivor arrested her! Handcuffs and all!"

Ivor laps it up. "Yes, yes, well.... It was just one of my little roles. And I sing and dance of course! I am what we know in the trade as a 'triple threat'! Alas, now I must tend to my trunk."

With that, Ivor turns and heads for the door. On hearing the first notes of the song he pirouettes and sweeps back in, causing Edith Rose whiplash as she wakes with a frightful start. She swoons! Ivor glides over every inch of space without a wheel on it, singing slightly off key but with the flair of Gene Kelly. Some of the lyrics are new to me but they seem to fit. Mostly. A couple of residents mouth the words, not enough breath to push out a sound but they are content with being a part of Ivor's silent backing group nonetheless. Our duet is a great success, despite Ivor finishing several very loud bars ahead of the music and me. He finishes with a deep bow. Swooning Edith has hardly dared breathe; from rapture or whiplash I am not sure. Gloria says quietly: "His son will come. But he won't take him out.

Never takes him anywhere, just stares at the clock and counts the minutes."

"And my head I'd be scratchin'
While my thoughts are busy hatchin'
If I only had a brain..."

One of the brightest residents is named Joy. She is bedbound so doesn't get much interaction except with the staff who all adore her. Once a month I pop in and catch up. We sing a couple of songs and then she chats about anything and everything just to have the company. I'm teaching her the song 'If I Only Had a Brain' from 'The Wizard of Oz'. She thinks this is hilarious but hasn't learnt more than two lines in six months. Today she tells me about her nightmare:

"Did I tell you that last night I swallowed the clock? The night before that it was a necklace my first husband gave me...fake pearls on cheap string. And on Sunday I swallowed the brown cane chair that used to be on the porch. It got stuck in my throat and woke me with such a start I leaned out of bed and tried to cough it up on the floor. Awful nightmares. The choking wakes me up. The only person I've ever talked to about it – the choking – is – was - my sister. With her usual air of I-couldn't-give-a-fuck she said it was obviously fear of something in the future. I said you're wrong about that because I don't think about the future. I don't let myself. It comes in waves. The choking. I was the pretty one, you see. Everyone said it. Which is why my sister secretly hoped one night I'd swallow Blackpool Tower. "Cough that up if you can!" Sibling jealousy. It's a killer. She's dead now."

She asks me to hand her the paper she's been writing on. It's some kind of official form.

"Here, I found this! I've been filling it in just in case they come. First name: Joy. Not worth the bother really is it? JOY. My mother's idea of passion. In a moment of otherwise prolonged depression her pills kicked in and there I was. Identified. Named. I made a point of scowling every time my mother introduced me. "Oh well...perhaps she'll grow into her name!" they said. I didn't. Previous medical conditions: Tonsilitis. Hernia. Mumps. Measles. Jaundice. Appendicitis. Arthritis. Hiccups. They wouldn't stop! Days. Weeks. My couldn't-give-a-fuck sister creeps into my room in the middle of the night while I'm having a nightmare about me and David Bowie doing a duet on "Britain's Got Talent" in front of forty-six million viewers and she leans over and shouts "Boo!" Never let anyone tell you giving someone with hiccups a fright will cure it. A heart attack, yes. My sister had to call the ambulance. The ambulance man gave her such a lecture about her moronic behaviour! She said she didn't give a fuck and went back to bed."

She adds a final note to the paper with a triumphant slash of the pen:

"Haemorrhoids!"

"High on a hill was a lonely goatherd
Lay ee odl lay ee odl-oo..."

I set off for a new care home today. Carolyn, the Activities Coordinator, meets me at the door. She looks panicked when I tell her I'm here to sing.

"Are you sure?" she says.

"Yes, Tuesday", I confirm.

"Oh, alright then but come on, come on!"

I explain that first I need to park my car.

"Well, there's a garage around the corner. The door is open so just park there. Go on, hurry!"

I find the garage with much difficulty. The door is indeed open but the garage is full to overflowing with old wheelchairs, bedpans, cots, walking frames and anything else that's good for tripping over. I walk through the garage to find Carolyn standing in the back garden looking bewildered. She looks at me, trying to work out where she's seen me before.

"They shouldn't be left on their own. Can you hurry?"

I catch up with her in the lounge where there are three severely disabled residents, drugged to the eyeballs.

"We'll start here for now. Can you visit the rooms and sing to the others after this? I haven't got time to bring them all down in the lift. Here we are, everyone, this is the singer I told you about, remember? This is Mona. She can't hear a thing so can you move a lot? Wave your arms about. And this is Anne. You like singing don't you Anne? Well she will when you start. Go on then! They like something bouncy. 'The Lonely Goatherd' is bouncy. It's a pity you don't have a ukulele.

'The Lonely Goatherd' is lovely with a ukulele."

I don't know 'The Lonely Goatherd' nor do I play the ukukele so I make do with a bouncy 'Que Sera Sera' and hear Carolyn's disappointed sigh. She pulls out her phone and starts taking photos of the poor unsuspecting residents. The much younger man in a wheelchair is trying to pull the head off a stuffed giraffe.

"Aren't we going to sing today, John? Mmmm? He's got a good voice believe it or not, haven't you eh?"

Mona has a bone to pick with the lampshade and Anne is staring at her jigsaw, waiting for it to do something. Mid-verse Carolyn heads for the door.

"That'll do. We have to visit Daphne. Come on, come on!"

I grab my things and run down the hallway after her. Daphne is bedridden, lying in a cot surrounded by huge bolsters. I have to peep over the side to see her properly. Carolyn pats her on the head.

"What would you like to hear, Daphne? Something not too morbid. Have you got a love song? Well, anything really, she won't understand, she's Belgian." Again, mid-verse Carolyn moves towards the door.

"She's had enough now, that'll do. She's tired. Come on, come on we need to see Arthur! He'll want something romantic."

The bleak, narrow room smells bad. Arthur is squeezed into a corner, propped up in an armchair, watching television with no sound. Carolyn perches on the bed and shoves me forward. There's nowhere to sit but on the arm of Arthur's chair.

"Sit there with Arthur so I can take a photo! This is the singer I told you about, remember Arthur? She's going to sing for you. What would you like?"

"Don't know," mumbles Arthur, not taking his eyes off the television.

"You're a bit of a romantic aren't you Arthur? Do you do Dusty? He'd like Dusty, wouldn't you, Arthur?"

"Don't know."

"Petula? Arthur? Hmmm? Petula?"

"Don't care."

On the television Bing Crosby is crooning to a nun.

"No, I don't have any Petula or Dusty," I say. 'How about 'Try to Remember'?"

"That'll do," sighs Carolyn impatiently.

I'm perched on the chair with Arthur, Carolyn's snapping photographs, and as I sing about life being slow and oh so mellow, I find I'm sitting right over Arthur's open commode. As the room starts to spin Carolyn interrupts again. "That'll do! Come on, we need to go upstairs!"

Arthur is confused. He remembers, perhaps, that 'Try to Remember' used to have more verses but Carolyn's already down the hallway impatiently punching the lift button.

"Oh, you'll love my next man! Brian. He's not well today but he was watching Lulu on television this morning and smiling. You do Lulu, do you?"

"No."

"That's a shame. Elvis?"

"No."

A heavy sigh. "I'll have to leave it to you then. Here we are! Hello Brian, how are we? This is the singer I told you about, remember?

She doesn't do Lulu or Elvis, which is a real shame."

I'm so relieved to see Brian's commode is covered I make myself comfortable but he starts to cough. Thick brown phlegm oozes from his mouth and I concentrate hard on the painting of a rhinoceros on the wall. Brian is coughing uncontrollably now. Carolyn pockets her phone. "It's your perfume! It's making him cough! Come on, we'll go and see Pat."

Off we race down another hallway.

"Really? My perfume?"

"Yes. We don't wear perfume here because it upsets them. Hello Pat! How are we? This is the singer I told you about, remember?"

Pat is sitting by the window, knitting.

"No, you didn't," she pouts.

"Yes, I definitely told you, Pat. Pat loves to tease, don't you Pat? Never mind, what song would we like? She doesn't do Lulu or Dusty, sadly."

"Or Petula," I add, just to annoy her.

"No. No, she doesn't do Petula either, which is an awful disappointment isn't it? What shall we sing?"

"How about Doris Day? 'Moonlight Bay'?"

"Oh, we love a Doris, don't we Pat?" says Carolyn setting up a publicity shot of two knitting needles.

Pat actually does seem to enjoy it. She knits in time too. But Carolyn can't resist an interruption. "I wonder if Dorothy's back in her room?"

Pat's needles click click click furiously and Carolyn senses the tension.

"Come on, we'll go and see Dorothy."

No time to say goodbye to Pat, who comes to the end of the row as her solo rendition of 'Moonlight Bay' dies a fading death. We run! This place is a rabbit warren. Carolyn knocks softly on Dorothy's door. Nothing. She knocks again and peeks in.

"Dorothy? How are we, Dorothy? The singer's here I told you about. Would you like to have a sing-song?"

"Drop dead, stupid woman."

Carolyn closes the door very gently. "She's not herself today. We'll go back downstairs and you can sing another one in the lounge. It's honestly a shame you don't do 'The Lonely Goatherd'. 'My Favourite Things'?"

I pretend not to hear.

"I take singing with them in the mornings," Carolyn says with a competitive air. "They love anything Julie. Here we are, Mona, the singer's back! Anne, you can finish the puzzle later. We're all going to sing again, isn't that exciting?"

Out comes the phone. Snap snap.

I sing 'Que Sera Sera' again with great difficulty as Carolyn is so loud and out of tune it's hard to compete.

"Oh! That was jolly wasn't it, everyone? I think we should have a big round of applause!"

Anne is still staring at the puzzle waiting for it to move. The giraffe's dismembered head lies on the floor beside John's wheelchair. John's asleep and Mona hasn't quite decided whether she agrees with the lampshade.

"Thank you for coming. They really enjoyed it. Next time I'll get them all down to the lounge. You should think about the ukulele you know, it's such a handy instrument. In the mornings I do a tambourine. It goes down a treat."

"No matter what the future brings
As time goes by..."

Beautiful Sheila died. As soon as I see her empty chair I know. She's always there. Day after day, morning till night. She loved company and couldn't bear to stay in her room alone. Sheila was one of the happiest ones and had the sweetest smile of all, with lips like little rosebuds underneath an expansive smear of coral lipstick. She was often asleep when I arrived but as soon as I started singing she'd wake up and quietly sing along. Sheila had always wanted to see The Carpenters as she'd collected all their records in the 1970s and was a huge fan. She loved Karen Carpenter and once, when we were talking about how tragic it was that Karen had died so young, Sheila said she had tried to book for their concert in Brighton many years ago but she couldn't get a ticket.

"Probably because Karen was already dead," she said.

"Some things that happen for the first time,
Seem to be happening again..."

Peggy is standing in the conservatory watching the clock on the wall. She's wearing a woollen coat and beret and holding her handbag. The clock strikes three and the little door swings open. A bluebird pops out, bobs its head up and down and disappears again. Peggy looks around, lost, then shuffles over to the chair next to Meera.

"I can't remember the number bus I get. It stops right outside my house. I want to go home," Peggy says quietly.

Meera loves to have someone to talk to. I've heard this story many times but I never tire of listening to Meera's enjoyment at telling it.

"When auntie died my cousin, Anjani, came around to our house to tell me. She was furious. She'd gone to pick auntie up and take her for a drive, which is something auntie hated because she said it was like driving with Mr Magoo. But to Anjani's great irritation auntie was dead in her armchair so she couldn't go on the drive and Anjani had wasted a trip. One time Anjani took auntie to a lunchtime concert at the church on Gully Hill near our house. The vicar asked if she'd be kind enough to pick up three other pensioners who wanted to go to the concert. Anjani didn't want to do that of course and she was in such a bad mood as she picked them up one by one. By the time the third lady had climbed in the back seat there was so much chitter chatter going on in the car my cousin couldn't stand it. She stopped the car half way up Gully Hill and stomped off in a sulk, leaving the three ladies wondering if they should have caught the bus after all. They said to auntie that they didn't know a person as rude as Anjani so auntie told them to get out of the car. She said Betty Cox could stay in the car because Betty was in a wheelchair and auntie worried about her being on a steep hill. Just as the ladies were fighting to get their umbrellas up Anjani came back. "Okay", she said. "One more peep out of you and I swear to god I'll do the world a favour and drive this car off the top of Gully Hill straight into the cemetery!" They never said another word."

Meera lets out a great guffaw at her own story as Peggy, who hasn't heard a word, stands up.

"I'd like to go home now." She checks her handbag and walks to the hallway. Meera calls after her:

"There's a few in here that aren't right in the head!"

The Mafia girls have their heads buried in Soduku and crossword puzzles. I pop in to say hello and offer to take them out for a coffee (it would give the nurses a welcome break, not to mention dear Betty!) but they don't want to go.

"No, we're alright here. We all used to go out in a big van but it got too expensive, Mr Barber says. We don't go anywhere now. We went to a garden centre a few times but what do we want with plants? Where are we expected to grow plants? It was a waste of a ride! Nice cuppa, I suppose." Fi goes back to her Soduku.

Maggie says: "We could pop into mine for a coffee if you like?"

My dog, Fred, is a great favourite with the residents and I take him to most of the homes. As soon as she spies us Coral bounds over. The conversation is a race to the finish:

"Darling! How wonderful to see you! Who's this wee fellah?"

"This Is Fred. How are you Coral?"

"Isn't he lovely! What's his name, darling?"

"Fred."

"Who does he belong to then?"

"He's my dog."

"Isn't he lovely? Bertie is it? Where have you come from today, darling?"

"Brighton."

"Oooh I love Brighton! I used to live there! Who's this little chappie?"

"Fred."

"How marvellous! Have you come far?"

"Brighton."

"I've never been to Brighton. Love to go some day. I'm Coral. I worked for the BBC. Forty years in documentaries. Forty years. But I prefer it here you know. People are nicer. I think this little fellah belongs to Jean."

"You must have some good stories to tell, Coral."

"Forty years and one marriage was enough! Derek. Ghastly man. Double-barrel whatsit. Hated my cooking. Johnstone-Thompson can you imagine? BO-RING! BO-RING man! He's dead now thank god. It's so lovely of you to visit, darling. Are you going to sing for us?"

"Yes."

"I'll take the little fellah back to Jean. Come on, fellah."

"Let's chat before I leave."

"Perfect, darling! I hope they bring the tea soon. Toby! Come!"

"High ho if love were all..."

Winnie sits at the window with her face to the sun, eyes closed. She looks so peaceful I don't like to interrupt but she smiles when she senses me at the door and seems delighted to have the company.

"Splendid! What are you going to sing?"

I suggest a song by Noel Coward.

"Perfect. I adored Noel Coward."

To my delight, Winnie knows this rather obscure song and hums along with me. She tells me she used to sing with a show band on cruise ships.

"A very long time ago. On the Cunard line from Southampton to New York."

She sees my surprise and laughs.

"Quite. I'm very old now but I used to have men trailing behind me, all declaring their undying love. I was quite an attraction in those days. They weren't looking for romance, though. Just a pinch and a tickle. My granddaughter wouldn't stand for that now!"

"Yes, things have certainly changed," I laugh. "For the better I hope."

Winnie thinks about this.

"Do you think so? I don't think my granddaughter is any happier than I was. She picks men to pieces, not a good word to say about any of them. I worry for these young men because I don't think they know how they're supposed to behave anymore. Mind you, I always preferred men who were a little feminine. There were lots of them working on the liners. Got up to an awful lot of mischief but I did enjoy them! I've lived ninety-three years and never found anyone more entertaining than a homosexual."

There's a lot of activity in the lounge today. An Elvis Presley impersonator (Dougie) got his days mixed up and is here a week early but insists that he's in the right and refuses to leave. Bevan, the Activities Coordinator, tries to explain that I'm down to entertain today but Dougie has had his costume dry cleaned and white boots polished, not to mention the pricey makeup and petrol he'd be wasting if he turned around and went home now.

"I can't just pop Elvis back in a box, you know!" he says. "I can't turn him on and off like a tap, it's art is this."

Sweat is beginning to form on Dougie's pricey makeup and the residents are arguing with Bevan that if the real Elvis Presley had come all this way (a few doors down the street for all they know!) he wouldn't dare turn him away. Poor Bevan is no match for Dougie or the residents and he watches helplessly as this beer-bellied Elvis bends over and switches on his amp, the zip in his white pants groaning in an effort not to split. I don't mind the mix-up as I'm free the rest of the day so I ask Dougie if I can sit in for a bit and watch. He's clearly thrilled to have a bigger audience but asks me not to join in, as it's a "finely tuned act". The volume is thunderous and the body moves are quite frankly obscene so I guess he assumes the residents are all deaf and blind. Some of the women titter, some look nauseous, but Ex Police Constable Harry Smith joins in, in full magnificent voice. At the end of the song Dougie purses his lips and says, "Boys and girls, Elvis Presley was a solo artiste so I hope you won't be offended if I ask you to refrain from your warbling unless invited to do so."

There's a momentary pause as this sinks in. Then a deeply offended Ex PC Harry Smith snaps.

"Listen sonny, my wife and I were singing in the Hull community choir before your voice broke, so don't come marching in here in your high heels and tell me not to sing! I've seen fellahs like you all my life, most of them locked up for lewd behaviour, too. So, you watch what you do in those tight pants of yours, there are ladies present. All right?"

And with that Ex PC Harry Smith gets up and leaves the room. Dougie tugs at his pants that have ridden up his arse and mutters into the microphone:

"Somebody's pea soup didn't agree with him at lunchtime, did it?"

The audience is very quiet for the remainder of the hour. Dougie swaggers and bawls.

"Join in you lot! I won't bite! What's wrong with you? Come on, wakie, wakie!"

Later Bevan tells me he won't be having the Elvis impersonator at the home again. Twins Barb and Mo said they hadn't been aware that Elvis had such a temper but perhaps it was on account of the alcohol. "Whiskey," they said. "He smelled like Daddy on a Friday."

"Fly me to the moon
and let me play among the stars..."

Dear fragile Dotty tells us that people at the Baptist Church in Crawley, where she attended every Sunday, used to mistake her for Shirley Bassey. She lightly dabs her pink cheeks with a hanky.

"I couldn't see it myself."

Mrs Pearce shouts, "You don't look anything like Sheilagh Fraser!"

Dotty adjusts her wig and smiles demurely. "There were that many requests for 'Gold Finger' I couldn't keep count. She was a very nice person, apparently. Shirley Bassey."

I tell her that Shirley Bassey's alive and still performing. Dotty leans forward and whispers,

"You know, you should phone her and tell her you're singing her songs. She should really be paying you for keeping her famous. Frank Sinatra too. They should be grateful."

I say it would be a bit hard to phone Frank Sinatra as he's been dead a few years now.

"That's sad. And him still in the navy."

Molly confides in her visitor

"I got lost while I was out for a stroll on Monday and had to knock on the door of number 27 to ask where I was. I must have looked a sight because the woman asked me in for a cup of tea. I felt like asking for a lie down too but I didn't think that was appropriate considering I'd never met her before and didn't know if she had a spare bed anyway. Isabelle – that's her name – lives on her own like me. We had a lovely morning talking about the bastard council and the old bridge, which is how I got lost in the first place. She had this beautiful egg timer in the centre of the dining table sitting on a plastic doily with all its edges curled up. I said "What a pretty egg timer! Very turn of the century from a far-off country." She says, "Oh that. That's my husband William in there." "There wasn't much of him!" I say. "Must have been a little bloke." "He was," she says. "Most of him ended up in the vacuum cleaner. He came home in a little box and the lady that does my feet knocked him off the book shelf so we had to vacuum him up. What's there is what we could save. Toenails and Ginger's fur in there as well but I don't think he minds." Isabelle and I arrange to meet up for tea in town one day. She arrives dressed to the nines. She's wearing a hat that's too small for her head and pulls her face back like she's facing a hurricane. I don't say anything. I'm trying to understand her eyebrows. They look like tadpoles drawn on in black crayon by a blind person, one higher and shorter than the other, and I swear to goodness they belong to someone else. Gives me vertigo staring at those eyebrows. Puts me off my muffin too so I leave only I can't find my street. Funny, it used to be that I couldn't find my glasses."

"If you're happy and you know it clap your hands..."

Riverside is the biggest and most exclusive home I go to. It's like a very posh hotel with several receptionists seated behind silk flower arrangements, a café serving turmeric lattes and organic cupcakes, and a bar in the foyer dominated by a Steinway grand piano that presumably gets played occasionally. Everyone wears a name badge and a smile. I can't imagine how much it costs to be resident here but I notice how well dressed everyone is. There are certainly no dressing gowns in the lounge. There's an aura of privilege and expectation that life shouldn't be any different in here from what it was on the outside: the evening gin and tonic, linen napkins and gardens tended by people in uniform.

I'm shown into the lounge by one of the receptionists who has been instructed to communicate in a whisper at all times.

"Do you need a power point?" she whispers.

"No, I'm fine," I whisper back.

"A glass of water?" she whispers.

"Thank you," I whisper.

On her return with the glass of water she whispers to a few of the residents who all smile and whisper in reply. A robust looking woman wearing a smart trouser suit approaches me and says very loudly,

"I hope you're going to be entertaining! If I leave it's because I don't like your music. Do you play the ukulele? We love a ukulele."

Often at these homes they don't join in the singing very enthusiastically, if at all. The smaller places are sometimes family run and it seems the residents are happier to join in. Well, that's an enormous generalisation of course, because at one of these small homes sits a man called Rodney whose face I've never seen. From beginning to end I observe a perfect Still Life: from underneath a newspaper gripped by eight white gnarled fingers sprout two knobbly knees clothed in a pair of woollen pants that wither and vanish into two tartan slippers. There is no page turned, no tut-tut, not a breath. Apparently, as soon as I'm signed out Rodney folds up the newspaper and switches on the tele. He hates music. This is his protest.

This morning I notice a new "art work" on the wall. It's as though it's been done by a remedial group for four-year olds, with cut-out shapes glued on to a piece of A2 paper creating a cow in a meadow. Each piece has been painted a dull brown or lifeless green, except for the cow's lips, which are a sickly pink as are the meadow flowers.

Rita sees me looking at it and says,

"Isn't it awful? I wouldn't have put it on my wall at home so I don't see why I have to look at it here."

A couple of other residents chip in with similar gripes and one-eyed Phil shouts from behind his Daily Mail,

"Bloody picture! We're not special needs patients! Bloody irritating woman!"

Apparently, a local volunteer named Pam comes once a week to do group creative activities ranging from rainbow rolling pins and jellyfish weaving to insect pompom balls and glitter saucers.

"We don't really enjoy it," moans Freda. "Pam's a nice enough woman but she talks to us as though we're not right in the head. All the projects are so juvenile. We're not allowed scissors unless she's supervising."

Phil shouts even louder, "And why should I want to say hello to a bloody guinea pig! That bloody woman brought along a bloody guinea pig last week as though it was the rarest animal known to mankind and passed it around for us all to say hello! I've not slipped into my bloody second childhood quite yet so I wish she'd bugger off and leave us alone!"

One of the resident's daughters is visiting and says to her mother,

"Oh, I think you enjoyed making that cow, didn't you Mum? You said you had a super time!"

"No I didn't! I made the tail and I think it looks ridiculous. It's not even been stuck in the right place. And look at the eyes, they're wonky and ugly and we shouldn't have to stare at it all day like it's a blooming Picasso!"

"I don't know why, when we're perfectly capable of having an adult conversation and still love to read a newspaper or go to a museum, why we should put up with this?" Rita says.

There is a young woman barely out of her teens who takes an activity incorporating music and ball games. While she sings along to a backing of "If you're happy and you know it clap your hands" she throws a ball to the circle of painfully arthritic hands and cries "Awesome!! You caught the ball!" If this was the World Cup for Imbeciles she couldn't be more excited, and when the ball can't be thrown back because Polly or Sid have no movement in their arms or possibly no arms, the young woman squeals "Oh it doesn't matter, dear, does it? The purpose of the game is to *try* to participate!"

Why start ball games at eighty-five when you hated them at ten? And when do we become "dear"? When a person half my age starts calling me "dear" I shall slap them. Hard.

Ivy

"I couldn't say how long I've been living here.
Time means nothing now. When my
husband was alive I relied on the clock day
in day out, week in week out. I suppose it
was to keep the routine: his job, dinner, bed,
make the house nice, church. It never
changed from one year to the next so I knew
where I was. Well, except if there was a
celebration, you know, like the birth of a
grandchild or a death, that sort of thing. I
relied on the seasons too. You have to if
you're a gardener. Autumn's my favourite. I
don't notice the seasons here because I
rarely go out. There's a garden but the staff
makes such a huff and puff about getting us
out on the lawn that by the time we're all out
there the clouds have come and it's time to
be wheeled back in. There's a rose garden in
the front I noticed one day when we were
getting on a coach to somewhere - all pinks -

and I thought: I must remember to come out and smell them one day. But I never did. I suppose they bloomed again this year. Deborah's left Rupert. Or he's left her. I don't know what's going on because she doesn't tell me much and she hasn't taken me back to hers for a long time. Probably embarrassed she hasn't got a husband anymore. It's not something to be proud of is it? I don't know what I'd have done without my husband, truly I don't. He gave me a purpose in my life. My children used to tell me off, especially Deborah. They'd say I was an idiot being his slave and why didn't I respect myself more? But I liked my life. I've always looked after people. I feel that's why God put me on this earth. Now I hate my life when I think about it and there's not much else to do *but* think about it in here, I can tell you. I hate it here. God forgive me but I'm so angry with my husband for dying. If he were still alive I wouldn't be here."

Deborah, her daughter

"I need this problem like a hole in the head but I think I'll have to find Mum a new home. My brothers are no help, are they? So I suppose it'll be up to me to organise it again. I know I'm being mean but Tom, my eldest brother, could at least try to cope, couldn't he? He's always been the sensitive one in our family and now if you mention visiting Mum he has a meltdown. "I'm not built for watching people decay!" he says. But I'm expected to soldier on while my marriage falls apart and my mother's accused of making the other residents cry. I don't know how much to believe because Mum categorically denies holding anyone in a headlock. The manager has suggested another home might suit her better but if she's terrorising people here it's only going to happen somewhere else, isn't it? She's lost a lot of weight so I am worried about her. I don't think she's given this place a good go, really. She's been here eighteen months and seems to have made no friends or joined in any activities. She's even stopped doing the crossword. I never saw the anger in Mum before; it was always Dad who scared us with his temper. But I see it now in Mum. She's so – well, so angry.

I don't know what to do."

"It's the hap-happiest season of all..."

It's December and Christmas songs are sung over and over and over again! For a few weeks now I've asked the residents if they're looking forward to Christmas.

"I hate Christmas."

"What's there to look forward to?"

"It's just another cold miserable day as far as I'm concerned."

I arrive at the first home this Christmas eve where they've gone all out with the decorations. There's a tree with wildly flashing lights that will likely have a dangerous effect on some, and lots of photos of former Christmases to remind everyone how many residents have passed away since last year. The lounge is festooned with tinsel and stars dangle over the large circle of sleepy residents who are wearing paper hats and clinging to balloons. Bernard's not wearing a hat and isn't holding a balloon. He's a big, bad tempered man with the added weight of all the negativity in the world on his shoulders. Today he's in a real grump. He's half sliding off his chair and there's a distinct whiff of alcohol.

"I'm dying and no-one cares! The pain's unbearable!"

Amy, who is in charge today, sighs and texts furiously as she whines, "The nurse saw you this morning Bernard, and she said there's nothing wrong with you."

"What would she know? I'm dying, I tell you! What would she know?"

I offer him a chocolate.

"No, I can't eat that! I'm too sick! Are you trying to kill me, girlie?"

"Why don't you just relax and enjoy the singing, Bernard? It's a party!" says Amy still texting.

"He's a miserable bugger!" shouts Mrs Adams from her wheelchair.

"I don't feel like singing! And you shut up, you nagging witch!"

I launch into a festive "It's the Most Wonderful Time of the Year" and a few in the circle join in. Bright paper hats slip down over tired eyes and forgotten balloons sail across the ceiling.

"I'm going to my room!" Bernard heaves himself up and limps across the room, weaving in several directions. He must have been at the sherry since lunchtime.

Amy shrieks at the hilarious text she's just received and hasn't noticed Bernard criss-crossing the room. Suddenly he crashes against the door and the full force of his weight flattens poor Ida who chokes on her Kit Kat. He clutches his stomach.

"I've been shot!!" He slumps to the floor. "Aaaaah!"

Amy sighs again, her thumbs never missing a beat...tap tap tap... "Where have you been shot, Bernard?"

"Aaaaah!"

Mrs Adams turns to me:

"I hope he doesn't find where I hid the gun."

"May your days be merry and white..."

Later I visit one of my favourite homes. Every one of the residents is fast asleep. A family of four sits on hard-back chairs staring at Iris who is rigid in her wheelchair and, I suspect, only pretending to sleep. Iris doesn't like visitors.

"She looks better than last time," one of the relatives says.

"Oh yes, much more colour in her cheeks," adds another.

"She must be eating solids again," remarks a third.

"I was so worried about her, you know," sighs the fourth.

"This is why I don't like company!" snaps Iris, eyes still closed.

The four look embarrassed that not one of them has anything more interesting to say.

"Would you like us to go now, Grannie?"

"Yes, perhaps you need your rest."

"It's been a big day, Mum."

"You've probably eaten too much."

Iris lets out the biggest fart humanly possible and revives half the room.

"Oh dear," says the younger man.

"Grannie!" shrieks the granddaughter.

"Mum, did you have to do that?"

"Too much fruit pudding," says the elderly man.

Iris grins triumphantly, leaning forward to release a second fart.

"We perfect them in here. When you get to my age it's the only ammunition you've got! I can clear a whole room in thirty seconds. Now, scram! I want to sleep."

The poor family scramble to their feet and make their farewells. No response.

Mr Turnbull announces to no one in particular that Nurse Roth is a German spy and needs to be watched carefully. He says she reminds him of spies he'd met on many occasions in his role as Benjamin Disraeli's Foreign Secretary and that Nurse Roth bears an uncanny resemblance to that notorious, monstrous spy, Vera Lynn. Mrs Birchall chips in that Vera Lynn was here only yesterday and she agrees the resemblance is indeed uncanny.

Although there'll be no joining in from the residents, I sing Christmas carols and the staff sings along. "White Christmas" wafts through the air and now and then there are odd words or notes snatched from somewhere long ago.

"I love this song," one of them says. Another adds, "I remember my dad singing this. Better than Bing Philby he was." "No, they don't write songs like this anymore."

As I pack up today and head off for my family Christmas, Alice makes a beeline for me, her walking frame knocking aside everything in its path. She beckons me close and whispers,

"Congratulations. I'm off home now. I'll take a taxi, it's quicker."

She presses something sticky into my hand. A half-eaten Licorice Allsort. Before I can say anything, she heads over to Happy.

"Congratulations, Happy. I'm off now."

Happy shuts his eyes.

"Fuck off you daft cow!"

Que sera sera...